SYLHETI HERITAG

Hazrat Shahjalal's
MAZAAR SHARIF

MAYAR AKASH

Publisher

MA PUBLISHER

Mayar Akash

Published by MA Publishing
www.mapublisher.co.uk

First printed 2017
All photo are taken by Mayar Akash

ISBN-13: 978-1-910499-03-0

Cover designed by Mayar Akash
Cover photo by Mayar Akash
Typeset in Times New Roman

Dedication

I am dedicating this book to my father, who in his last days of his life wiped away all the emptiness I had of him, with his love and protection he gave me and represented; when I was vulnerable and fragile.

I am also dedicating this book to my sister who sadly passed away before I was born and that void couldn't be filled. I miss my sister and she has always been in my prayers, during the good and bad times.

I would like to dedicate this book to my life, what it has been for me, and who it has made of me.

Life, living has shaped my world and I'm beginning to now understand, where I am getting at?

It has taken lives to grow me; souls to mould me and time has stretched my sense to mature me.

For what it's worth I dedicate this book to my souls' that slipped out from my life.

Mayar Akash

Acknowledgment

My journey began in the UK and when I travelled to Bangladesh, I didn't expect the journey it turned out to be. It became my spiritual journey and I travelled to the Mazaars, and for that I would like to thank my late father Al haj Mashuk Miah, my mother Asiah Khatun and my older brother for financing me and my journeys.

I would like to thank the late Soraqum Ahia Kobir Ahmed Kuti Miah who was then the Secretary of the Dorga, for giving me access to the Mazaar Sharif with the assistance of his son Sonnet. I would like to thank Soraqum Mohammad Bahulul Kobir (Sonnet) for taking me into the family and personally assisting and facilitating me in and around the Mazaar.

I thank Mufti A.A Nojomuddin Ahmod (LLB) for allowing me access to the Sword and taking pictures at his residence.

I thank Soraquome Usuf Amanullah, who was the Moutowalli (Trustee) of the Dorga for giving me permission to have access to the shrine and taking pictures. I am the second person in the history of the Mazaar to be allowed to take pictures.

I would also like to thank the drivers who took be around all over Sylhet and Moulovi bazaar who I trusted my life with. The first driver was Abdul Bari (Faruk) and the second was his younger brother Khalique.

And all the people who have supported me throughout my journey to put this project together.

Mayar Akash

CONTENT

Introduction

I am a typical Bangladeshi living in London. I have lived in the UK all my life, brought up in the East End of London; Shoreditch, Tower Hamlets. I grew up during the eighties and didn't understand the effects and social impact of the policies that where shaping me.

The changes such as political changes, shifts of local power and resources to homes and services impacted on my parents and this filtered down to me. My parents like many parents could not focus on the material luxuries in life during the 80's such as colour TV or a front loaded VHS video or spinning washing machines but we made do with what mum and dad could afford.

Other social issues that impacted us were the racial changes and prejudices that existed in "pockets" in and around our lives. There were constant fear of racial abuse and attacks on people and their property. Services, facilities, food and entertainment were limited at the time. The local community maintained a close nit relationship and enjoyed a community unity spirit, where voluntary organisations were set up to help the community with the emerging issues.

This has had a huge impact on my identity and of the future generation. The community didn't know or understand, in the early to mid 80's but look at us now. This identity crisis amongst Sylheti young people has come about various struggles within it as well as outside of the community, at all levels.

This is evident in our community and society; new identities have fused with integration in each generation. Majority of the Sylhetis' who came from Sylhet are Sufis. The mainstream religion in the UK has over ridden, diluted the beliefs and practices that our ancestors had, however this still existed with our parents who came over and were the first generation in UK.

The Sufi identity is not promoted or practiced openly by the Sylheti community in the UK but many parents, the senior members of the first generation and their sibling still continue to maintain the traditions in Bangladesh.

The Sufi tradition still lives and thrives in all over Bangladesh. It is clear that all who return to Bangladesh, whether for holiday or longer term stay ensure on their itinerary a visit to Hazrat Shahjalal's Mazaar Sharif.

This is a knowledge that I've grown up with, that my parents upheld the practice and contributed financially for its upkeep back home in Bangladesh. My parents did not involve me or my young siblings however, my elder sibling financially contributed.

Now, I realise that this "behind the scene activity and event" was and is a major part of my history. It became "behind the scene activity and event" as a result of the mainstream middle east Wahabi Islam in the UK. It has been displaced due to practise and propagation of mainstream religion which dwarfs the Sylhet Sufism.

So after three and a half decades later, and as a young person who climbed the ladder of the youth service by becoming a youth and community worker, it has given me firsthand experience in all aspects of the growing life in the UK; issues that affected the community run through my life and blood.

My life took a turn and I went on a soul searching mission to Bangladesh and spent about 12 months, soaking up the community, traditions and culture. This included a major part of travelling around Sylhet, to the Mazaar (shrines) of the Sufi Saints, the main one being Hazrat Shahjalal in Sylhet Dorga (mausoleum).

During my time in Bangladesh I managed to visit 250 shrines throughout Sylhet, and parts of Moulovi Bazaar and Dhaka. Of the visits to 250 sites there were approximately 500 shrines and mausoleums.

This has been a spiritual, personal, social, educational, religious and humanist development journey for me. I have photographed and documented all the visits that I made. I made it a point to try to visit all the 360 Auwliyah (Saints) that came to Sylhet with Hazrat Shahjalal. The 360 Auwliyahs were sufi practitioners who joined Hazrat Shahjalal on his journey from middle east, Turkey to India and then on to Sylhet, Bangladesh. It wasn't possible to visit all the Mazaar but I have managed 70 authentic sites.

I have produced a range of "Sylheti Heritage Collections", for the young people of the future generation of Sylhetis' to have access to information and knowledge and preserve the roots.

In these books I will be giving an in-depth view of Hazrat Shahjalal's Mazaar in Sylhet and the traditions and customs that are still alive today. I also hope that I am able to clarify to the generations of young Sylhetis as to why it is a must to visit when visiting Bangladesh.

I've produced pictorial guide to the shrines, the relics, the estate and those who manage it. I am proud to say that I am the second person to be given permission to photograph the shrines and

11

the preceding processions and the Urus (commemoration). I was given the privilege to photograph one of the management families of the shrine, who gave me a personal tour and explained their rituals and rites they hold and practice.

This experience was an eye opener for me and allowed me to understand firsthand my heritage. Meeting the family who are descendants of members of the 360 Auwliyah, who up keep the traditions practiced from the times of Hazrat Shahjalal and preserve rituals and the customs. It certainly opened my eyes to many social issues that we have in the UK; that doesn't exist in the practices of the faith in Sylhet. The issues in UK are; such as integration of men and women in participating Sufism, restricted practices and the lack of promotion of Sufism.

The estate does not publicise or promote Hazrat Shahjalal and his shrine officially, this is my personal endeavour to bring it to the attention of a forever diversifying and integrating fusioned group of people in the UK.

This book is intended to preserve the history of the Sylheti heritage, numerous books are available in Bengali but not in English. This is geared for the young and old of all communities who are English speaking and anyone who wants to learn.

The Attractions

The Shrine

Men and women attend the Mazaar Sharif to pay respect and ask for help and support. Non Muslims are not allowed up in the tomb upstairs but are allowed to be in the Mazaar complex for contemplation and prayer, and check out the features as follows.

The Fish pond

It is a spectacle to see the fishes come up to the surface and give you a stare. They also expect to be fed as this is a common practice. There are small huts with fisher men/women selling a plate of small fishes, these fishes also eat meat as they are carnivores.

The Pigeons

Pigeons are another attraction as the original pigeons were given to Hazrat Shahjalal himself by Hazrat Nizam Uddin and brought them over with him from Indian.

Feeding time is also a spectacle as the crowds gather and the pigeons flock to feed.

The Degs

These degs were donated by the mogul in the 1600AD to the Mazaar Sharif and it has been in the Dorga ever since. The pots are used as for donations and alms. People put their money inside the pot and it holds quite a bit of cash.

The Well

The Well was originally dug by Hazrat Shahjalal to provide water for the new Muslims to wash, bath and do ablution. It still exists and its maintained and recently modernised. Adjacent to the well is a fountain where you can see golden Koi fish. This has been an attraction for centuries and the water from the well supplies the water. Just outside the fountain enclosure is another watering hole that was used for bathing and washing for the Muslims. In it too you will find golden Koi fishes. In both the places it is not a frequent sight for the golden fish, so if you see it, luck is on your side.

The Sillah Khana (Contemplation room)

In the inner sanctum of Hazrat Shahjalal's tomb is the Sillah Khana (contemplation room). This is a space that the Shah used to contemplate and meditate.

Non-Muslim will not be allowed to this, visit or see the Sillah Khana.

The Three Domes

This is another attraction that the Moutowalli of the Mazaar Sharif did not knock down the old mosque to build the new five storey mosque that the Mazaar now boasts. They build another mosque around it and on top of it. They have retained the old mosque by encapsulating it in the 5 story mosque.

Non Muslims can see this attraction by asking the office, this can be facilitated by the office during the times outside of the prayer times.

Lighting candles

You can light a candle and incense sticks all around the complex, there are spaces, spots allocated, set aside and on top of the walls. You can buy these candle in the parades of shops in the street leading to the Mazaar.

You can visit www.mazaar.org.uk for more information about the Mazaar Sharif and the history.

THE MAZAR

Mayar Akash

The Estate

Here we are going to look at Mazaar Sharif as a whole.

The estate is looked after by the Moutowalli (trustee) of the Mazaar Sharif. They look after and maintain the complex and its amenities.

The estate covers many acres of land, consisting of the Mazaar, the mosque, the burial grounds, the ponds, the Kua house, the residence, the office building

In the site map you can see their locations.

- Dorga Gateway/The main entrance/exits
- The main mosque/The five storey mosque
- The Madrasha
- The Courtyards
- Ladies room
- Burial grounds
- The Orphanage (Etim Khana)
- The White domed mosque
- Steps leading up to the shrine
- The Shrine
- The Sillah Khana
- Pigeon house
- Degs
- Gozar pond
- Fountain, Well & Pond
- The 3 domed mosque (inside the 5 storey mosque)
- Ostrich Egg
- Moutowalli (Trustee)
- The Minaret

Diagram of the Estate

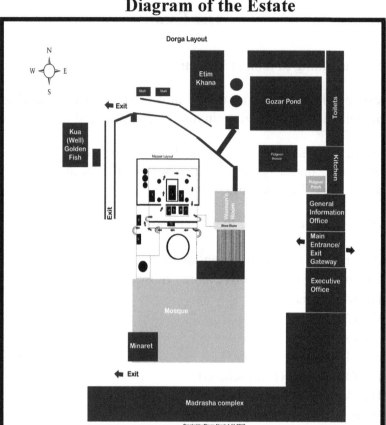

Mazaar Sharif Layout

I created this diagram as an overview of the estate. The scale and the details are not accurate or current. This visual overview is for information purposes only. This map is not official or endorsed by the Mazaar management or the estate.

This is to visualise the estate and make some sense of the different parts and location. The map and layout are subject to change.

Dorga Gateways

This is the sight that greets you at the other end of the Dorga Moholla. By the time you get to this point, you will have passed many of the shops selling various artefacts, incense, to candles, books, perfume, sweets, shinnee, white sugar candy, stones, jewellery, clothes and much more.

What you can do here?

You can now do all your tourist shopping there, book a hotel room and enjoy a whole host of restaurants.

<u>Caution! Beware of children begging! if you give to one rest of the dozens will not leave you alone, they will harass and hound you. Wait</u> till you have finished what you needed to do and then after you have boarded your transport, and then give it through the window. It's tough if you are in a rickshaw as they will run behind you. Anyhow if this is something you are ok with then good luck.

The other side of the main gate

This is the day time view of the main entrance/gateway in to the courtyard.

Other gates around the Mazaar Complex

Doriya Road Entrance: The stars that decorate the structure is very pleasing to the eye. I had to stop and take in the splendid design artwork.

This is the entrance gate to the back of the tomb of Hazrat Shahjalal. This is also the pathway to the local graves. Again the architecture took my interest. The double columns, the symmetrical design and the colour, its pleasing to the eyes and the mood, its inviting, calming and less congested.

The five storey mosque

This is the view of the mosque and the court yard, it's very calm and you can see men, women and children visiting and also note there is no presence of overbearing guards. There are volunteers who maintain order but there is no authority or force projecting any presences. This is the "Order of the shrine", it is a place of peace, tranquillity, contemplation, prayer and offerings and all are welcome.

This is the view from the top of the 5 story mosque looking out to the Dorga Mohollah.

It's quite refreshing coming down from the rooftop and you see over the Mazaar complex as well as into the Dorga Mohollah, the road, estate leading to it. From this vantage point one feels that significance of the religion and the significance of the shrine and the impact it has on the people, community and the environment.

This entrance leads out to the court yard and I found this exit/entrance interesting and I tried to compose an image to capture the symmetry. I was fascinated by the designs and architecture and use of shapes and lines.

I want to give a visual feel of the complex through these composed shots, also the height of the landing overlooking the top of the canopy also gave me the feeling of the care and attention being paid to the devotees that attend the shrine.

What you can do here?

This is a place of contemplation and if you like architecture, shapes and symmetry then this is a place for you to sit and let your eyes and mind enjoy. It's not a wow architecture but I'm easily pleased as my objective is peace, tranquillity and harmony and I found all of them from this place as well as other parts of the Mazaar.

Not only does the shrine provide the setting for devotees to come and pay their respects and pray, the shrine complex also has a school known as a Madrasha where children come and learn Arabic and do quranic and hadith studies. These out building are located in the courtyard.

Mazaar is also an educational establishment, providing educations for local, national and international students, as well as the orphans that reside there.

What you can do here?

From this height you can see the courtyard and out into the horizon. Just enjoy the view, the lush greenery and it doesn't matter what ever the weather it is soothing

Maintain etiquette at all times.

27

Court Yard

This picture of the courtyard made me sit down and soak in the tranquillity. Outside the mosque, the iron frames spanned from one side to the other with date trees giving shade and breeze; and the marbled floor. The shade of colours also added to the mood and atmosphere and also the warm heat of the season, could sit there forever. There is no restriction or limit to sit and contemplate until it's the prayer time.

For tourist & Probashi
Remember, if you are not use to the sun & the heat, make sure you put on suntan lotion. The heat from the sun is high in the Mazaar as it reflects off the white marble floor and the walls.

What you can do here?

You can sit and relax and infuse the calmness and serenity of the place. Be sure to get a shaded place and or under the palm trees. Don't get sun burnt.

Again this is different perspective from the court yard facing towards the pigeon house, a vantage point where you can see the entrance to the shrine.

I just couldn't get enough of the date trees, the greens of the tree tops on the backdrop of white tiles, building walls and blue sky.

29

Women's quarter

The women's quarter is the building on the right hand side, a single storey with the three arch way. There, women can sit and meditate, contemplate, pray and have access to water for ablution and to use the toilets.

Here we see more foot flow and we see a greater mix of people.

What fascinated me is the non segregation of the grounds of the courtyard. However, females are not allowed up the steps to the tomb of Hazrat Shahjalal.

All men and women are to maintain modesty at all times, covering the body from ankle to their head from women and ankle to their shoulders for men. A skull cap is worn by majority of the people automatically.

What you can do here?
You can take photograph and film in most parts of the Mazaar Sharif but not in Hazrat Shahjalal's tomb enclosure.

Burial grounds

Dorga ground level, there are other burials that can be seen. These tombs are of the family members of the shrine keepers

These graves are of the descendants of the companions and are significant but not more than Hazrat Shahjalal. During the various events that happen over the year people attending it will make duah and prayers to Hazrat Shahjalal and will include all the graves in the complex, thus these graves get acknowledge through it.

Also their descendants will offer prayers during their respective death dates.

These are private burials and low maintenance.

The Orphanage

The shrine complex also houses an orphanage. In this picture we can see the orphanage on the right hand side. The Mazaar Sharif provides for orphans and takes care of their welfare.

The proceeds from the shrine and donations directly from the people accommodate many orphans of the town and country. The Mazaar Sharif maintains their duties to the community and to support the development of the society that the shrine is part of.

The Mazaar Sharif continues to support the community as Hazrat Shahjalal begun his life in Sylhet the 14th century. His legacy is maintained by the trustees of the Mazaar.

The White Dome Mosque

This is the view of the iconic white domed mosques on top of the steps. This picture is taken from inside of the 5 story mosque. You can see the canopy to Hazrat Shahjalal's tomb.

It is surrounded with lush green tree which provides shade during the sunshine and breeze. This adds to the peacefulness, the serenity and tranquility of the inner sanctum of the shrine.

This is the mosque building on top of the stairs, the entrance to the shrine is through this building to the inner sanctum of the tomb of Hazrat Shahjalal.

What you can do here?

Here you can pray, read, contemplate, purchase candles and incense sticks, get a parcel known as Tabaruk, inside it has white sugar candy.

With Tabaruk you take this back with you. Tabaruk is symbolic of the Mazaar and the blessing from the shrine. You make intention and take it back home; you take a piece of the Mazaar with you.

Similar to "rocks" sugar sticks you buy at the seaside and other tourist places in Unites Kingdom and other places in the world.

This is inside the white domed mosque on top of the steps and the walk through to the Hazrat Shahjalal's shrine.

What I was fascinated with was the architecture of a single dome and one room with arches and doorways. As you enter, the dome opens up and engulfs you. The atmosphere and the energy in this room is so tranquil, the calmness settles you.

What you can do here?

Sit and relax and during prayer times take part. Truly a chilling out place as its cool and serene, with the fan blowing air when it's hot.

Adjoining court yard which leads to Hazrat Shahjalal's Mazaar also leads to the graveyard of other people and dignitaries who have been buried around the mound. One such dignitary buried there is Coronal Atwal Goni Osmani who led Bangladesh to liberation in 1971.

Here you will find the black tablets are with inscriptions. They are painted with the red borders and are now kept behind the fence.

There is no part of the upper sanctum of the Dorga that doesn't commands peace and tranquillity, with the canopy of the tree tops and the secludidness by the walls. The white walls and the marble floors create the cleanliness and an inviting feeling of serenity and contemplation.

The candle light at night adds that mystic side to time and the compulsion to wish/prey upon a flame/light. The candles are lit to represent souls and guiding light for the spirits.

Mayar Akash

38

The Shrine

Map of Mazaar layout

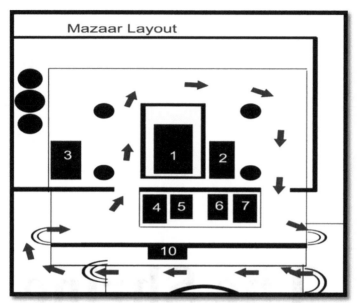

Here is a blown up of the Dorga layout of the inner and the main shrines.

As a tourist there I wasn't sure who the others were and why are they there, and what was their relationship with the Shah.

No.1 is of Hazrat Shahjalal.

No.2 is of Shahzada Sheik Ali (Prince from Yemen)
Sheik Ali travelled from Yemen to follow Hazrat Shahjalal and that what he did and he died in the Dorga. He was a beloved of Hazrat Shahjalal and was his aid support.

No.3 is of the Governor of the Dorga, Soyod Mokbul Alom (Uzir Mokbul Khan). He looked after the Dorga and took control of servicing the Mazaar and the people of the time.

No.4 is of Haji Doriya

Is another companion of Hazrat Shahjalal and is buried adjacent to this tomb.

No. 5 is of Haji Yusuf

Hazrat Haji Yusuf was another one of Shah's companion who became his Khadim. Hazrat Shahjalal chose him to assist him and look after his requirements. He must have died before Haji Doriya and before Haji Kholil & Haji Abu Turab.

No. 6 is of Haji Kholil

Haji Kholil is another one of Hazrat Shahjalal's trusted companion who remained close the him. And he is buried next to the other three companions and adjacent to the Shah's tomb.

No. 7 is of Abu Turab Abdul Wahab

Abu Turab was another one of his companions and remained loyal to him throughout Shah's life. He rests along with the other three trusted companions of Shah.

No. 10 Sillah Khana – contemplation room

Follow the arrows, you will come through the white domed mosque, into the court yard in the middle and then in to the shrine enclosure.

This is the shrine of Hazrat Shahjalal

This picture was taken with the permission of Soraquome Yusuf Aman Ullah , who is the Moutowalli.

This is the tomb of Hazrat Shahjalal, well maintained and cared for.

This tomb is very large, larger than the average graves and the ones surrounding it.   Hazrat Shahjalal was a tall man according to description given in Ibn Batuta's notes and the tomb proves it.

The tomb has gone through modernisation and landscaping as time has gone by. Here we have the area walled up and the floor of the whole Mazaar is marbled.   It is very clean and hygiene is maintained as cleanliness' is key to a Muslim and especially someone of Shah's standard when he was alive.

Caution! You are not permitted to take photographs in this space.

When you enter the inner enclosure you are greeted with the fragrances from the incense sticks and of the rose water sprinkled over the tomb, by the guide guarding the tomb and every individual devotees paying their respect.

People will lay flowers, reefs and drop money as a gift and or a prayer or a wish attached to them.

Devotees will make duah, prayer known as "Koybor Ziarot", but not limited to that. Many people will stand there and contemplate, meditate and do dhikir, silent chanting.

People also light up candles and incense stick around the wall of the enclosure in custom made spaces.

Note: you are not allowed with your shoes, or unclean (smelly or dirty clothes).

Inside the shrine complex

Wide angle view of the shrine from the far side of the

This is the inner sanctum of the Dorga that women and non Muslims are not permitted. This is a well maintained space, very clean and fragranced by the incense sticks. There is a vibration within the four walls that zaps any stress or anxiety.

You are received by the four shrines 4-7 as listed.

View of the shrine from the far end. You can see people saying their prayers around Hazrat Shahjalal. They are not worshipping him or his tomb, they are appreciating him and seeking gods attention through the contemplation.

Separate prayers are said as they enter the shrine through one entrance and out through a separate exit way, there is a foot flow system in place.

What you can do here?

Say your prayers, offer homage to the saint and take in the tranquillity, the serenity and let your mind and body relax.

45

Sheikh Ali

This is the tomb of Shahzada Sheikh Ali, on the right side of Shahjalal's. He was devoted to Hazrat Shahjalal and came over from Yemen to commit his time.

Sheikh Ali's grave is next to

Hazrat Shahjalal's grave, in very close proximity. Ali must have been very closed to Hazrat Shahjalal.

The close proximity to Hazrat Shahjalal's grave implies he was someone special, someone closest and dearest, nearest to a family member as Hazrat Shahjalal did not marry, so there is no family blood line.

Governor of Dorga

This is Soyod Mokbul Alom (Uzir Mokbul Khan) the Governor of

the Dorga and is buried on the left side of Shahjalal. The governor was also a Wazir, his tomb is also in the inner sanctum.

In this picture you can see the holes in the wall to light your candles. It is like that throughout the Mazaar complex.

Who is a Wazir or Uzir?

Wazir is someone who helps "carry the burden", but there are other definitions available. Here the Wazir/Uzir helped Hazrat Shahjalal with the governance of the land. "Uzir" is a regional dialect pronunciation of "Wazir"

From the location of the grave we can see that he had a very significant role and his importance. However he is slightly tucked away from Shahjalal's grave and from the other five.

His grave stone is fairly large as well; he must have been similar size as Hazrat Shahjalal.

Contemplation Room

This is what you see as you enter the complex, you can see the "Sillah Khana" on the right, centre.

This gated enclosure is known as the "Sillah Khana", it is decorated with this ornate gates.

This was a space where Hazrat Shahjalal spent time reciting, contemplating in isolation for hours. No one is allowed in there other than to decorate and clean. It is big enough to do sajida and stand up.

This Sillah Khana is the symbol everything that a Sufi is. Historically the Sillah Khana is where a true sufi spent most of his time connecting with god. A Sillah Khana is like a little cave, a hole, dark and with door or closing flap to lock oneself away from the world. This one is highly decorated by the love of the trustees of the Mazaar.

This is the place where one would go to forget about the world and worldliness and focus on god only, devotion to seeking god, oneness with the dark, blackness inside and merge with the blackness of sight and the mind. Recitation of the dhikir, poems and hymns as well as getting connected spiritually, let the source within project its light into the black canvas of the pitch dark cubicle ones in.

In there, it's just you, isolated, alone with ones love and that is god. get intoxicated in the invocation of the love for god and lose yourself in a trance.

Prayer space

There are prayer space up in Shah's tomb enclosure

The prayer rooms adjacent to the Mazaar of Hazrat Shahjalal.

This is where you can sit in the presence of the Shah and spend your time meditating, contemplating and praying.

Kobutors (The pigeons)

White pigeons coloured for decoration and festivity purpose.

The pigeons are one of the attractions at the Dorga and revered and favourite with the children.

Hazrat Nizamuddin Auwliyah of Delhi awarded Hazrat Shahjalal with a pair of dove.

Who is Nizamuddin Auwliyah?
*Hazrat Shaikh Khwaja Syed Muhammad bin Abdullah Al Hussaini **Nizamuddin Auwliyah** (1238 – 3 April 1325) also known as Hazrat Nizamuddin, was a famous Sufi saint of the Chishti Order in the Indian Subcontinent.*

Shahjalal brought them along with him to Sylhet and looked after them and they bred. The doves are still honorary residence of the Dorga. The doves are known as the "Jalali Kobutors", named after him. They are prized and looked after and there is a prohibition to eat them and also there is a fear of the wrath will fall upon whosoever was to kill and eat any.

As you can see in the pictures the pigeons are at home with the thousands that daily flock to Dorga making their spiritual journey.

It is also the case that those gifted doves have also integrated with the local doves and interbred. So it will be difficult to single out an original pair of the gifted pair.

People come from all over the world to see these Jalali Kobutors (Shahjalal's Pigeons) this is a very busy picture. I wanted to capture a piece of the Dorga with the pigeon and people getting along side by side

What can you do?
You can feed the pigeons.
You can wait for the feeding time and watch the whole flock come and eat.

You cannot catch nor kill or eat any pigeon as they are protected by the Mazaar and held sacred.

Did you know? His *nephew ate couple of the pigeons while Hazrat Shahjalal was away. When he leaned of that afterwards Hazrat Shahjalal banished him from the Mazaar and Hazrat Shah Poran set himself up in Khadim, where his Mazaar is still situated.*

This is one of the attractions of the Dorga feeding time of the pigeons.

The nearest experience I can compare to is Central London, Trafalgar Square, for those who've been to London (no longer has pigeons in Trafalgar square).

53

The Degs (Big Pots)

This is the biggest pot out of the three.

These pots are another attraction of the Dorga and there are three of them. The visitors donate by depositing money in them after making intentions and or charity.

These pots get filled up on regular basis with cash by visitors. Non Muslim also visit the shrine and pray and donate to the Mazaar.

These Degs were gifted to the Mazaar Sharif, dated 1106 Hijri, 12th Romzan (1695), by the Mogul.

[Aurangzeb Alamgir (1658-1707) was the Leader of the Mogul Empire. This information has not been verified by any officials that the degs were gifted by emperor Aurangzeb Alamgir himself.]

54

People from all walks of life and religion visit the Dorga, from all over the country and world. They make prayers and intentions and drop the money in to the pot, like a wishing well.

The Deg house is seen in the corner, pointed by the arrow.

The Gozar (Fish)

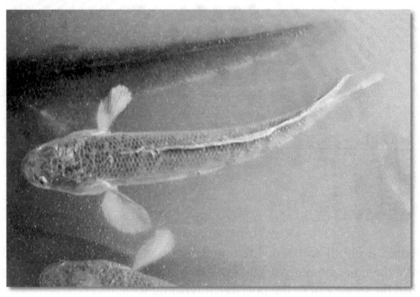

Gozar fish is a freshwater fish. This fish can be found in some Asian countries like Bangladesh, India, Pakistan, Thailand and some other countries. Canal, swamp, pond, small rivers etc are their main living place. Gozar fish known as various names in various places. It is also known as gozal fish, gazli, channa marulius etc.

Feed
Gozar fish are cannibalistic in nature. They are carnivorous fish species and eat zooplankton while baby. Adult fish eat snail, small fish, frogs, insects etc. Sometimes they also eat their own species.

These fishes are given a burial when they die because it is believed that these fishes posses human spirits. They are revered for those particular reasons.

This a day and night pictures of the fish pond. This is where the big fishes are found.

People also use the water to wash their feet, hands and their faces and some do drink it but wouldn't recommended to foreigner, you need very strong gut bacteria to deal with it.

Daytime view of the Gozar pond.

What can you do there?

For fish lovers this is a spectacle as you see many of the Gozars will surface to the top to see you. They have big eyes and what you will see is, big puppy eyes looking up at you from the water.

They also respond to voice, so have a go calling them, "madari, madari".

You can stand there and you will see the fishes swim up to the surface and also feed them small fishes that are available to buy around the pond. It's the interaction between the fishes and human being that is fascinating, intriguing and captivating, gives a sense of wonderment.

Kua (Well)

I was privileged to be around for the opening of the newly modernised Jhorna. This was very modern and like what we have in London and other developed countries. This was refreshing to see from the contrast of the old just outside its walls.

The landscaping, the lighting, the water feature, the ambience really made it a pleasant environment to spend some time soaking in the atmosphere and the history.

This is the original well that has been preserved, the top has been enclosed with a glass pyramid.

The history behind the well and what it symbolises. After things settled in the area and the Muslim community and population grew, the Muslims were still fairly small in numbers. There arose a social condition issue that there were no clean water for the Muslim community to wash, bath, ablutions and drink.

So Hazrat Shahjalal dug this well to address the social issue for the growing Muslim community. This was one of many of the social issues the Shah had addressed for the local people.

This is the original golden koi pool outside the fountain building and has been refurbished. This pool has been accessed by thousands of people over the years.

This is the pond adjacent to the well for community access for bathing and washing.

These acts have given Shah the social acceptance, recognition and respect. This social contribution has also showed fairness, and for the people, this will have an effect on the local people to convert to Islam.

This is the night time illumination of the Kua House

This was the first day when the fountain refurbishment and modernisation was opened to the public. I had the opportunity to photograph the freshness of the new opened excursion within the Dorga complex. This is another one of the attraction. In the pool of water the golden koi swims.

The water from the well is pumped through a fountain now into this modernised and landscaped pool.

Night time view of the well

In the fountain quarter it has a feel of an oasis, with the grey stone wall and the water in the middle. It is calm and the water trickling in to the pool sets the serene mood as well the warmth forces you to chill.

Here is what you can do?

If you're like me

- Relax and meditate or contemplate, if you don't mind the people.
- You can read/write,
- Draw/sketch,
- paint pictures,
- take photos.
- You can light candles as there are slots in the stone walls for that.
- You can just sit and watch the day go by, even though there are people there it is still tranquil and serene, this calmness just melts you away.

The Three Domed Mosque

The three dome mosque is now preserved and worshipers now are feets away from the building itself, a mosque inside another mosque.

The mosque has been preserved and maintained so that generations of devotees and worshipers can share its history.

The colour of pink and white gives a calm and relaxed atmosphere and soul warming feeling.

The three dome mosque is now enclosed within the 5 storey mosque. Worshipers can see it from each landings.

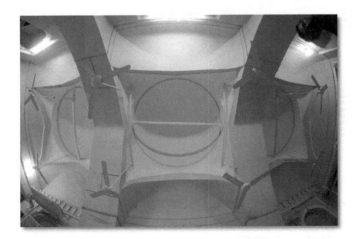

This a fly's eye view of the domes from inside of the mosque. It is an impressive structure with the thick two foot wide columns made of bricks.

65

I love what they have done to this building and how they have preserved it. The love, devotion and value jumps out to me, the energy it gives is awesome.

The Ostrich Egg

There are total of three ostrich eggs in the Dorga complex. This one hangs up in the mosque, on top of the steps.

The ostrich eggs were brought over by the Auwliyah as they journeyed through the Middle East.

The eggs are revered and great care has been taken to preserve them and it astonishing that they have lasted for so long.

Moutowalli

The traditions are maintained by the chosen one by Hazrat Shahjalal himself before he passed, his long trusted companion and khadim who entered Sylhet with him, Hazrat Hazi Yusuf.

We are now in 670 years on and the customs being fulfilled by the young generation while the world is modernising and technology changes all aspects of life even in the Mazar sharif.

Hazrat Shahjalal chose the person that was going to succeed him after his death. He chose his companion Hazi Yusuf as his successor and Hazrat Hazi Yusuf's descendants have been the custodian for Hazrat Shahjalal's Mazaar Sharif since his death in 1346AD, however Hazi Yusuf has been by his side since 1303AD.

As a result of Hazi Yusuf being personally selected by Hazrat Shahjalal to succeed him, the family have been bestowed the title of "Soraqum" and this title is not transferable to any other family,

Hazrat Hazi Yusuf's family have been managing the Mazar Sharif since 1346AD and this dutie has been fulfiled by Hazi Yusuf's decendants.

The trustees are descendants of Hazrat Haji Yusuf who was the Khadim of Hazrat Shahjalal. Hazrat Shahjalal chose Haji Yusuf to continue looking after the Mazaar and the estate. The title endowed is "Soraqum", this title means that they were the chosen ones.

Then there is the continuation of Khadims through Hazrat Haji Yusuf's linage, Gaddinshin Khadim, again "Gaddinshin" is a title endowed to look after the needs of Hazrat Shahjalal, of his tomb and his ceremony and work he started and died with.

Late Soraqum Ahia Kobir Ahmed (Kuti Miah)

In 2010 the Gaddinshin Khadim was Soraqum Ahia Kobir Ahmed (Kuti Miah) who sadly passed away after a short illness late that year. His eldest son took his place Soraqum Mohammad Bahulul Kabir (Sonnet).

So Soraqum Mohammad Bahulul Kobir inherited the Gaddinshin Khadim role from his late father, Soraqum Ahia Ahmed Kabir. This role puts duty on him to serve on everything to do with the Shah's personal requirements.

The other descendant of Hazrat Hazi Yusuf is the Moutowalli (the trustee of the Mazaar Sharif), in 2010 it was Soraqum Usuf Amanullah who was the Moutowalli current replacement is Foteh Ullah Al Aman.

This is a daily routine of the Moutowalli where those who are aware of him will acknowledge him with a salaam.

The Moutowalli of the Mazaar Sharif, Soraqum Yusuf Aman Ullah, is sitting in the courtyard and observing the devotees with his associates.

Both the titles and duties are passed down the family linage, father to son and so on.

Did you know? this has been going on for the last 670 years.

If you happen to be visiting during Asr time you will probably get to see him. Asr is the third prayer time during the late afternoon and before Magrib which is the night fall prayer time.

The Minaret & the clock tower

This is a close up of the minaret (Dorga) with the clock at the top of tower, another one of an imitation of the "Big Ben", the little balconies give it cuteness.

This is a view from the back street. This place is busy during the Friday prayers and many other times of festivities. The backstreet is less photogenic than the front, however the square minaret dwarfs the street. As always, beware of pick pockets.

Mayar Akash

Personal Artifacts

The Plate & the Bowls

These are the personal artefacts of the Shah, they have been set in a wooden box and glass casing. They are not displayed in public but get private viewing. They are managed by the owning families and not the Dorga committee.

The personal artefacts of Hazrat Shahjalal have been preserved and safe guarded by the families of the Dorga for the devotees to see.

The bowl and saucer are inscribed with quranic verse which he ate and drank out of.

The Sword

This is the sword "Torwal" of Hazrat Shahjalal.

I was just intrigued with the iron work on the sword handle. This is the dated back to the 1300AD, peice of history right in front of me and it is still being handled.

The Shoes, Clogs

These are Hazrat Shahjalal's personal possessions. The clogs made of wood and hard wearing. The wear and tear is visible.

The design fascinated me, the construction of the clog from one piece of wood and carved out of it, the height, its higher at the front and lower at the back, the technology of the times, it must have been muddy.

Just imagining how it would have felt wearing them?

The environment during Shah's life would have been muddy, horse, cattle and carts during the monsoon season and dry during the hotter weather. Having walked in the mud and soft soiled pathways and roads I can see the practicality of the design. In these pictures the toe pin is missing.

I'm wondering if the walking would have been slower or faster in the soft wet soil with those wooden clogs.

Mayar Akash

Jumma at Dorga

Jumma is a communal session where all the Muslims locally come together in a mosque to pray together and the Imam gives a sermon. This happens throughout the Muslim world on a Friday.

Performing salat on the rooftop of the 5 storey mosque praying under the green canopy, shade from the scorching heat of the sun.

Every Friday is Jumma day for muslims all over the world. I was there for my very first Jumma at the Dorga.

It was another item ticked off my list. I was with thousands of people in the Dorga complex taking part in the prayers.

In both pictures, people on the roof of the 5 storey mosque

Fridays are a busy day at the Mazaar. The whole complex is buzzing with energy and the spirit.

This is a view from the top of the 5 story mosque. This was taken after Jumma prayers on a Friday.

After prayers many people take in the view and also take selfies and pictures.

The people at the Dorga

Regulars, lining up for their daily alms offerings in the back street.

This can be an ordeal for the non suspecting tourist and it is recommended not to give to the beggars waiting outside as you risk being mobbed and hounded to pay and especially children, they will follow for miles, behind your vehicle. Many have experienced this and so have I, what seems like innocent becomes very distressing.

You can donate to the Dorga and that will get distributed down to the people in the form of shinnee (food parcels). For many of the beggars it is their occupation and they earn a living, they finance a very healthy living to their standards, where they fund their children's education, purchase rickshaws and rent it out as well as a comfortable and cosy home. As a result of this many beggars can be ruthless.

The true beggars are in the villages who by circumstance in life don't have any food to eat or money other than what they receive in donation and are known to the villagers.

To my astonishment I have learned firsthand, the beggar refuse your money, because it is either not enough or they want the £, some are not interested in your loose change. Yes you want to give, but soon as you give one you will be swamped.

I took the policy that worked for me it was that I will not pay anyone anything when I arrive to a location only when I'm leaving and when I know that I will not be returning back. However, if I know I'm returning back then I will not pay, only on the final leg of the trip or visit; otherwise they recognise you and will swamp you when they see you again.

I hope this didn't come across too brutal but you have to safeguard your safety and security yourself. You can learn it the hard way or take notes.

Alms seekers of the Mazaar

Women, men, children and families congregate behind the Mazaar for their daily share of the offerings.

Not all people here are alms seekers, some of them are visitors from different part taking an opportunity.

Did you know? Not everyone in the crowd is a beggar.

I promised them all that I will take them to London.

Cheeky chap wanted his picture taken. Oh look! I caught my toes.

Mayar Akash

Glossary

Al Mujarrad	The bachelor
Ashon	Camp
Asr	Afternoon prayer time
Auwliyah	Saints
Bast	State of mind
Darvish/Dervish (Persian)	The poor, beggar
Deg	Large pot/cauldron
Dhawq	tasting, trance
Dhikr	Remembrance, recitation
Dorga	Mausoleum
Fana	Annihilation
Faqir (plural: Fuqara)	The poor, beggar
Gaddinshin	Personal assistance/butler
Gozar	Name of the fish in the pond
Hadith	Collection of Prophet Muhammad's (PBUH) saying and doings
Hadhramaut	Region in Yemen
Hafiz	Title: when you learn the Quran by heart, memory.
Hal	State of mind
Hazi/Haji	Title given to those who have been Makkah, for pilgrimage
Hazrat	Honourable
Ikhlas	Absolute purity of intention and act
Jalalabad	Sylhet known as during the reign of Hazrat Shahjalal
Jalali Kobutors	Pigeons belonging to Hazrat Shahjalal
Jhorna	Fountain
Jumma	Friday prayers congregation

95

Kamaliyat	Enlightenment
Karimganj	Region in India/Bangladesh
Khadim	Caretaker
Koybor	Grave
Kua	Watering Well
Madari	A word used to call the Gozar fish in the pond at the Dorga
Madrasha	Islamic School
Magrib	Sunset prayer times
Mahabbah	Love
Makdoum	Title: attained once you learn the hadith of by heart
Ma'rifah	Interior knowledge, gnosis
Mazaar Sharif	Shrine/Mausoleum
Mohollah	Avenue
Moutowalli	Trustee
Mukam	Sacred Shrine
Murid	Disciple
Phagoleh doriliseh	Possessed
Probashi	Bangladeshis, living abroad
Qabd	A state of mind
Sajida	Prostration
Saksasor	Successor
Salafi	Islamic School of thoughts
Samri	Skin
Shah	Title: in Persian means King
Sharjah	The chain of
Sheik Gaht	It's a place in Sylhet
Sheikh	Title
Sillah Khana	Contemplation room/cubicle
Silsilah	The chain of /history

Sipha sala	Military person
Soraqum	Inherited title
Srihatta	Old name for Sylhet in Bangladesh
Suf	Wool
Sufi	Mystic
Tabaruk	White sugar candy parcel in a newspaper parcel, symbolising of the Mazaar
Tariqah (plural: "torus"	The path, the way, or the order
Tasawwuf	To dress in wool
Tawakkul	Absolute trust in god
Torwal	Sword
Wahabi	Islamic School of thoughts
Wazir/Uzir	Someone who "carries the burden"/personal assistance/ advisor
Ziarot	Prayer for the dead

Mayar Akash

Reference & Sources

1. http://www.roysfarm.com/gozar-fish/ - information about the Gozar Fish.

2. http://www.yanabi.com/index.php?/topic/207719-the-history-of-hazrat-shah-jalal-and-the-spread-of-islam-in-bengal/

3. http://hazratshahjalalyemeni.com/

4. http://www-personal.umich.edu/~vika/TeachPort/islam00/esposito/chapt2.html

5. http://empires.findthedata.com/l/46/Fatimid-Caliphate

6. http://hazratshahjalalyemeni.com/#4

7. https://www.britannica.com/topic/Sufism

8. http://www.religionfacts.com/sufism

9. http://gloriousindia.com/places/as/karimganj.html

10. http://maps.thefullwiki.org/Shah_Jalal

11. http://www.mazaar.org.uk

12. https://quran.com/62/10

Mayar Akash

Other Titles

by MA Publisher.

Published Titles

1. Father to child -
by Mayar Akash

This is a 116 page collection of growing up reflection in the form of poems. The central theme is about a person growing up, from being a child to fathering children and being aloof growing up to loosing contact with the children.

ISBN-13:9781910499009

2. Father to Child eBook-
by Mayar Akash

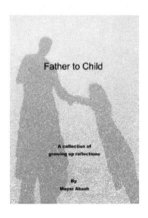

This title is available in the book format as well as eBook. The eBook is available from iTunes.

ISBN-13:9781910499023

3. Family Tree of Sheikh Chand –
by Mayar Akash

This is a private 114 pages publication for family members only.

ISBN-13: 9781910499016

4. Family Connection of Al-haj Md Mashuk Miah – by Mayar Akash

This is a private 592 pages publication for the family members only.

ISBN-13: 9781910499047

5. Tides of Change -
by Mayar Akash

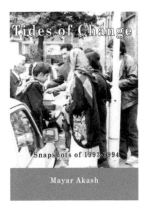

Tide of Change -takes the reader back more than two decades, to a time when the activities of the far right political parties were active in the Bethnal Green area of Tower Hamlets, London.

ISBN-13: 9781910499054

6. Anthology One
By Penny Authors

Anthology One is the title of the book by Penny authors. It has a collection of poems by different writer.

ISBN-13: 978-1-910499-15-3

For up to date information about all the publication catalogue please visit www.mapublisher.co.uk